DISCOVERING DINOSAURS

Protoceratops

Kimberley Jane Pryor

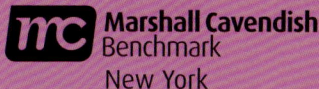
New York

This edition first published in 2012 in the United States of America by Marshall Cavendish Benchmark
An imprint of Marshall Cavendish Corporation

All rights reserved.

No part of this publication may be reproduced, stored in a retrieval system or transmitted, in any form or by any means, electronic, mechanical, photocopying, recording, or otherwise, without the prior permission of the copyright owner. Request for permission should be addressed to the Publisher, Marshall Cavendish Corporation, 99 White Plains Road, Tarrytown, NY 10591. Tel: (914) 332-8888, fax: (914) 332-1888.

Website: www.marshallcavendish.us

This publication represents the opinions and views of the author based on Kimberley Jane Pryor's personal experience, knowledge, and research. The information in this book serves as a general guide only. The author and publisher have used their best efforts in preparing this book and disclaim liability rising directly and indirectly from the use and application of this book.

Other Marshall Cavendish Offices:
Marshall Cavendish International (Asia) Private Limited, 1 New Industrial Road, Singapore 536196 • Marshall Cavendish International (Thailand) Co Ltd. 253 Asoke, 12th Flr, Sukhumvit 21 Road, Klongtoey Nua, Wattana, Bangkok 10110, Thailand • Marshall Cavendish (Malaysia) Sdn Bhd, Times Subang, Lot 46, Subang Hi-Tech Industrial Park, Batu Tiga, 40000 Shah Alam, Selangor Darul Ehsan, Malaysia

Marshall Cavendish is a trademark of Times Publishing Limited

Library of Congress Cataloging-in-Publication Data

Pryor, Kimberley Jane.
  Protoceratops / Kimberley Jane Pryor.
    p. cm. — (Discovering Dinosaurs)
  Summary: "Discusses the physical characteristics, time period, diet, and habitat of the Protoceratops" —Provided by publisher.
  Includes index.
  ISBN 978-1-60870-538-2
  1. Protoceratops—Juvenile literature. I. Title.
  QE862.O65P795 2012
  567.915—dc22
                    2010037188

First published in 2011 by
MACMILLAN EDUCATION AUSTRALIA PTY LTD
15–19 Claremont Street, South Yarra 3141

Visit our website at www.macmillan.com.au or go directly to www.macmillanlibrary.com.au

Associated companies and representatives throughout the world.

Copyright text © Kimberley Jane Pryor 2011

All rights reserved.

Publisher: Carmel Heron
Commissioning Editor: Niki Horin
Managing Editor: Vanessa Lanaway
Editor: Laura Jeanne Gobal
Proofreader: Helena Newton
Designer: Kerri Wilson (cover and text)
Page Layout: Pier Vido and Domenic Lauricella
Photo Researcher: Brendan Gallagher
Illustrator: Melissa Webb
Production Controller: Vanessa Johnson

Printed in China

Acknowledgments
The author and publisher are grateful to the following for permission to reproduce copyright material:

Photographs courtesy of: Corbis/Richard T. Nowitz, **29**, /Louie Psihoyos, **14**; Photolibrary/© Bruce Coleman Inc./Alamy, **8**; Photolibrary/Ray Nelson, **9**.

Background image of ripples on water © Shutterstock/ArchMan.

While every care has been taken to trace and acknowledge copyright, the publisher tenders their apologies for any accidental infringement where copyright has proved untraceable. They would be pleased to come to a suitable arrangement with the rightful owner in each case.

For Nick, Thomas, and Ashley

1 3 5 6 4 2

Contents

What Are Dinosaurs?	4
Dinosaur Groups	6
How Do We Know about Dinosaurs?	8
Meet Protoceratops	10
What Did Protoceratops Look Like?	12
The Skull and Senses of Protoceratops	14
Protoceratops Fossils	16
Where Did Protoceratops Live?	18
What Did Protoceratops Eat?	20
Predator or Prey?	22
How Did Protoceratops Live?	24
Life Cycle of Protoceratops	26
What Happened to Protoceratops?	28
Names and Their Meanings	30
Glossary	31
Index	32

When a word is printed in **bold**, you can look up its meaning in the glossary on page 31.

What Are Dinosaurs?

Dinosaurs (*dy-no-soars*) were **reptiles** that lived millions of years ago. They were different from other reptiles because their legs were directly under their bodies instead of to their sides like today's reptiles. Dinosaurs walked or ran on land.

At one time, there were more than 1,000 different kinds of dinosaurs.

Dinosaurs lived during a period of time called the Mesozoic (*mes-ah-zoh-ik*) Era. The Mesozoic Era is divided into the Triassic (*try-ass-ik*), Jurassic (*je-rass-ik*), and Cretaceous (*krah-tay-shahs*) periods.

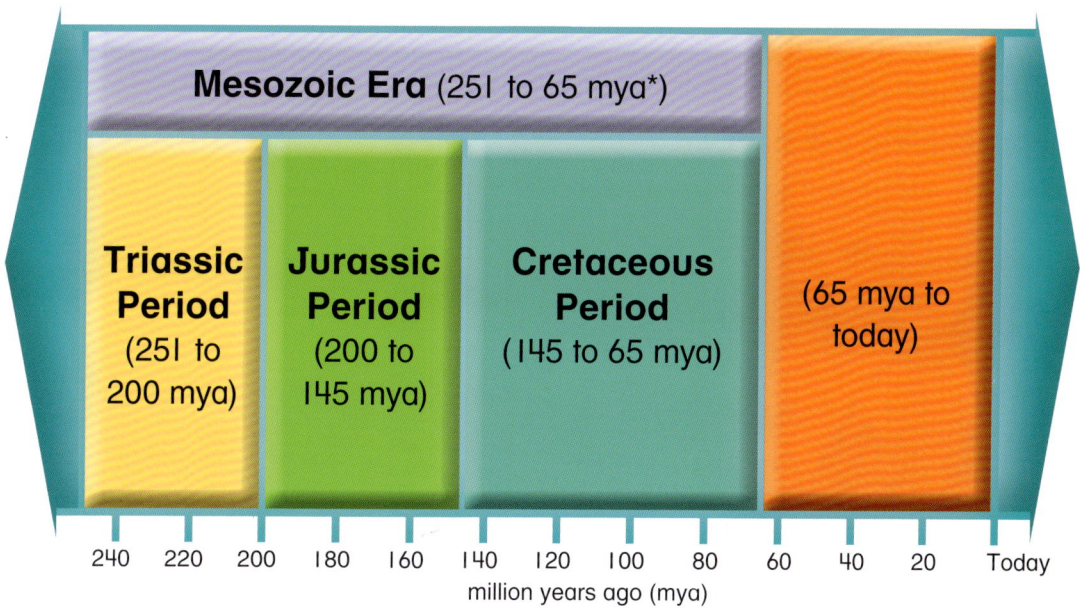

This timeline shows the three different periods of the Mesozoic Era, when dinosaurs lived.

*Note: mya = million years ago

Dinosaur Groups

Dinosaurs are sorted into two main groups according to their hipbones. Some dinosaurs had hipbones like a lizard's. Other dinosaurs had hipbones like a bird's.

All dinosaurs were either lizard-hipped or bird-hipped.

Dinosaurs

Lizard-hipped dinosaurs

Bird-hipped dinosaurs

Dinosaurs can be sorted into five smaller groups. Some lizard-hipped dinosaurs walked on two legs and ate meat. Others walked on four legs and ate plants. All bird-hipped dinosaurs ate plants.

Main Group	Smaller Group	Features	Examples
Lizard-hipped	Theropoda (*ther-ah-poh-dah*)	• Small to large • Walked on two legs • Meat-eaters	Tyrannosaurus Velociraptor
	Sauropodomorpha (*soar-rop-ah-dah-mor-fah*)	• Huge • Walked on four legs • Plant-eaters	Diplodocus
Bird-hipped	Thyreophora (*theer-ee-off-or-ah*)	• Small to large • Walked on four legs • Plant-eaters	Ankylosaurus
	Ornithopoda (*or-ni-thop-oh-dah*)	• Small to large • Walked on two or four legs • Plant-eaters	Muttaburrasaurus
	Ceratopsia (*ser-ah-top-see-ah*)	• Small to large • Walked on two or four legs • Plant-eaters • Frilled and horned skulls	Protoceratops

This table shows how dinosaurs can be sorted according to their size, how they walked, and the food they ate.

How Do We Know about Dinosaurs?

We know about dinosaurs because people have found fossils. Fossils are the preserved remains of plants and animals that lived long ago. They include bones, teeth, footprints, and eggs.

These fossils are the nest and eggs of a Protoceratops.

People who study fossils are called paleontologists (*pail-ee-on-tol-oh-jists*). They study fossils to learn about dinosaurs. They also remove dinosaur bones from rocks and rebuild **skeletons**.

dinosaur bones

Paleontologists carefully brush away soil from dinosaur bones to study them.

Meet Protoceratops

Protoceratops (*pro-toh-ser-ah-tops*) was a small, bird-hipped dinosaur. It belonged to a group of dinosaurs called ceratopsia. Dinosaurs in this group walked on two or four legs and ate plants.

Protoceratops had a large head and a neck frill.

Protoceratops lived in the late Cretaceous period, between 85 and 80 million years ago.

The purple area on this timeline shows when Protoceratops lived.

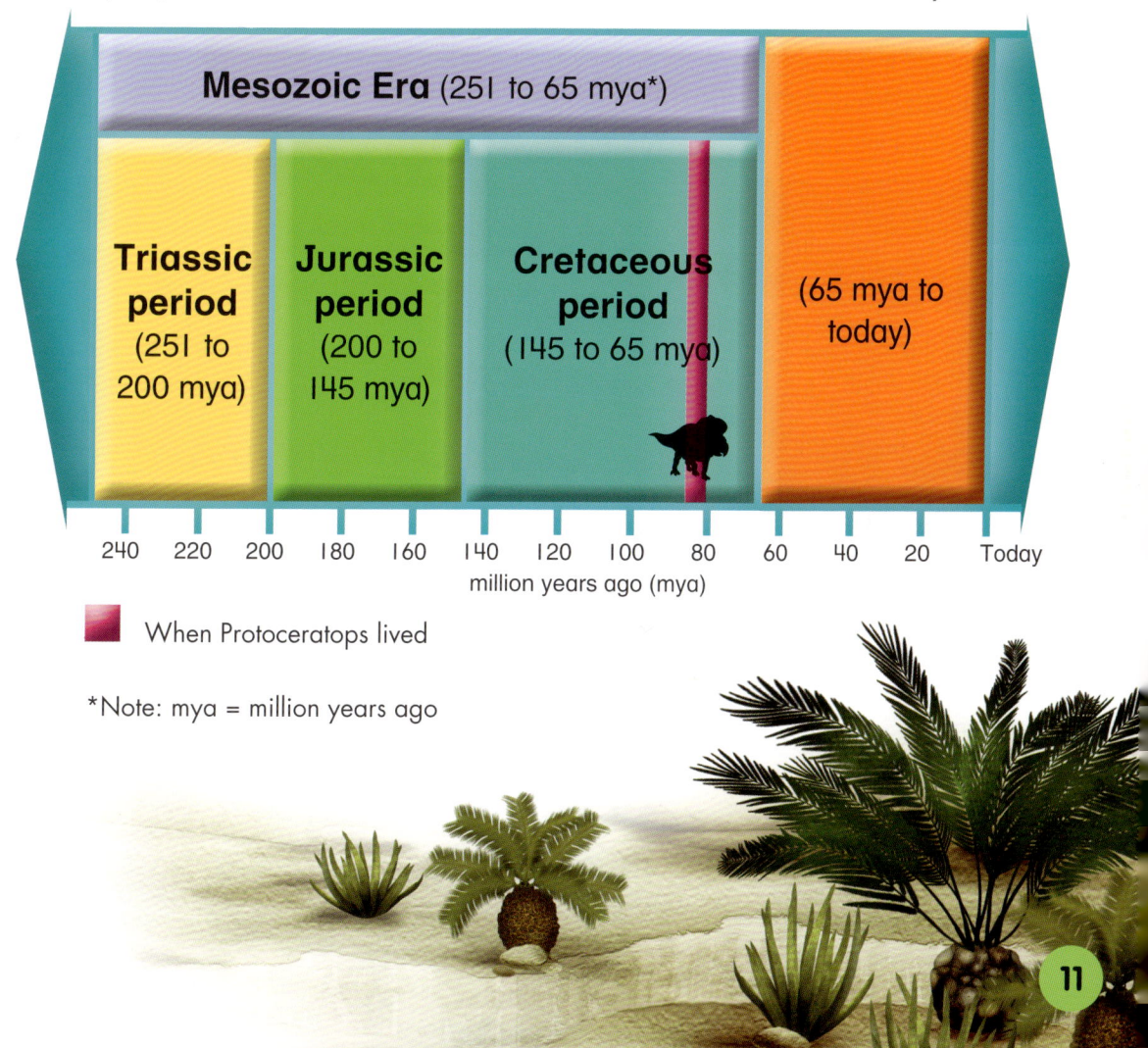

What Did Protoceratops Look Like?

Protoceratops was 6 feet (1.8 meters) long and 2 feet (60 centimeters) tall at the hips. It weighed up to 397 pounds (180 kilograms).

Protoceratops was slightly larger than a sheep and as heavy as a lion.

Protoceratops walked on four legs. It had a large head with a sharp, parrotlike beak and a neck frill. Protoceratops had a heavy tail. It probably had scaly skin.

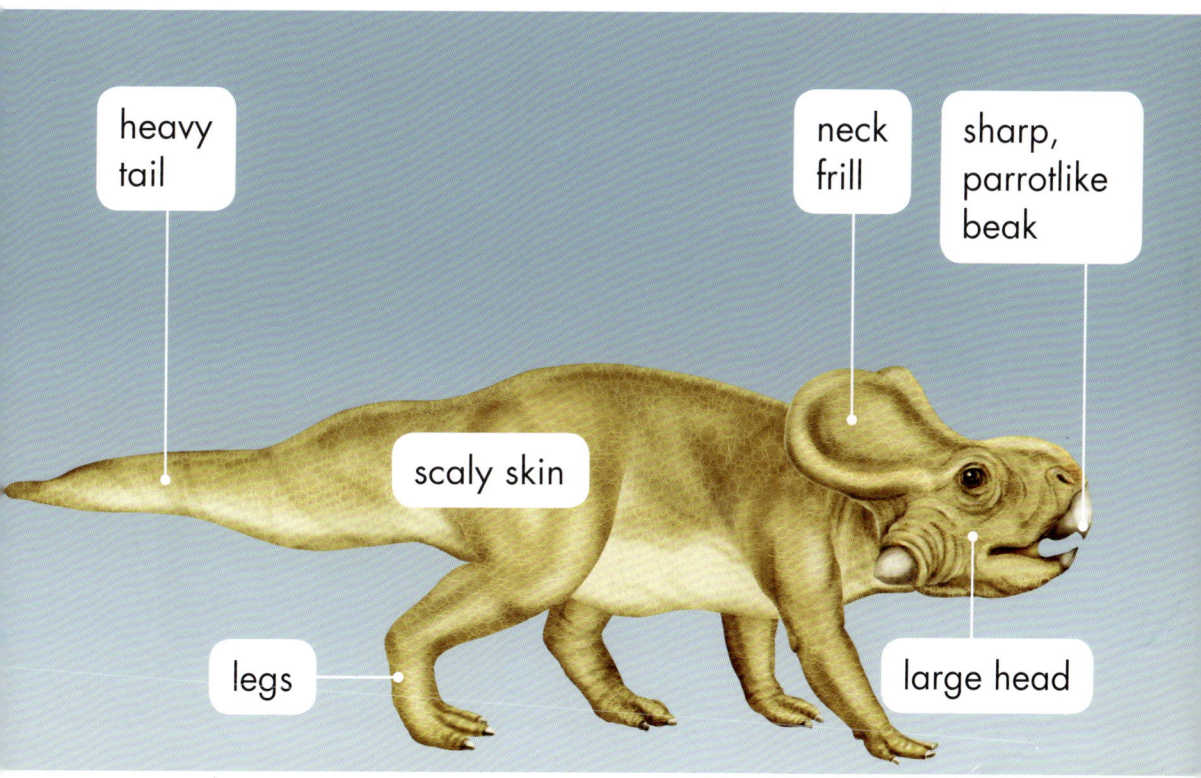

The Skull and Senses of Protoceratops

Protoceratops had a large skull. However, its brain was not large for its skull size, so it was not smart. The frill of Protoceratops grew faster than the rest of its skull!

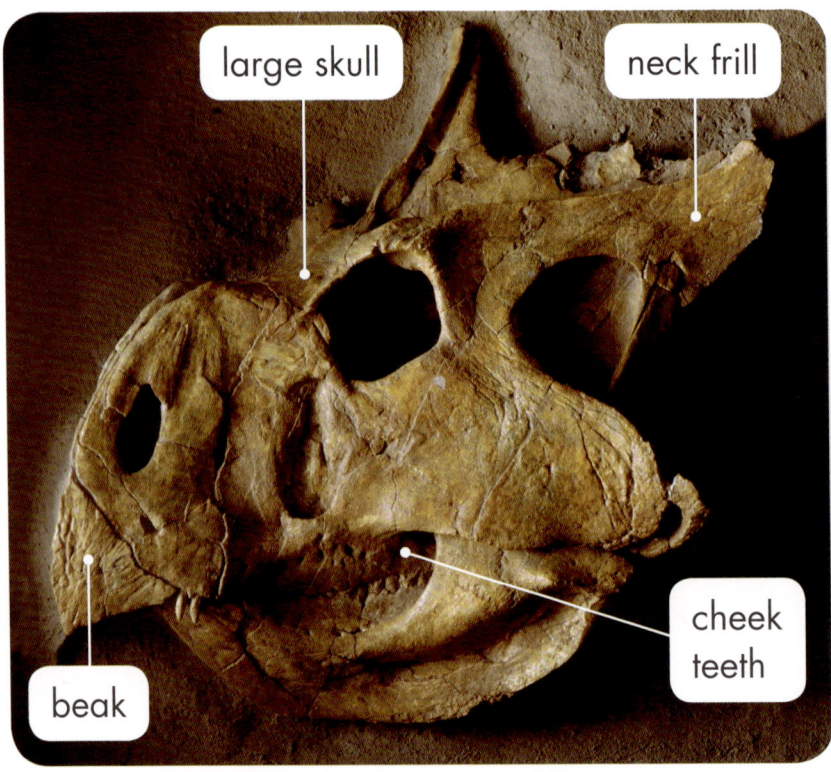

Protoceratops had a beak, a neck frill, and many cheek teeth.

Protoceratops could see well because it had large eyes. It probably had a fair **sense** of smell, which helped it find food.

The Senses of Protoceratops				
Sense	Very Good	Good	Fair	Unable to Say
Sight		✔		
Hearing			✔	
Smell			✔	
Taste				✔
Touch				✔

Protoceratops Fossils

Protoceratops fossils have been found in China and Mongolia, in Asia.

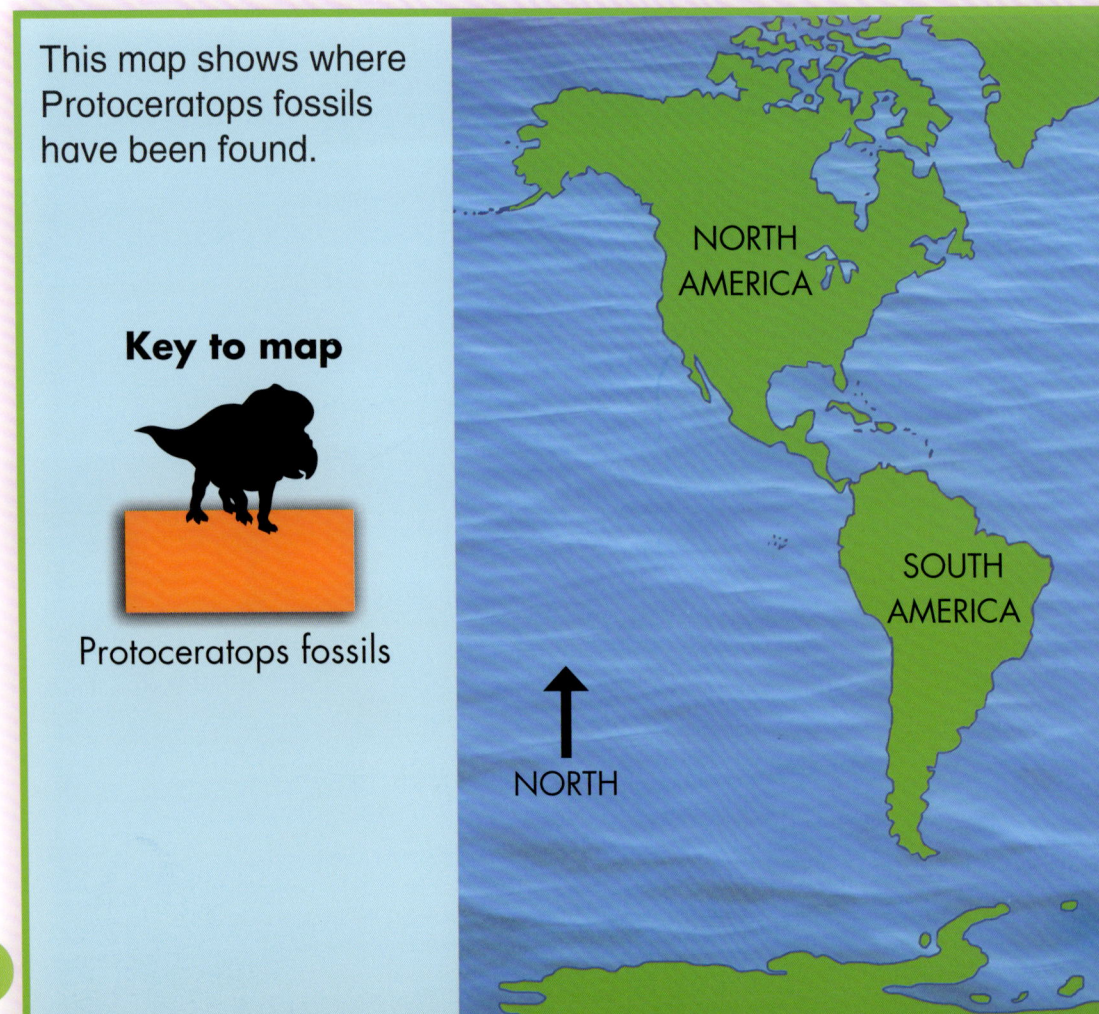

This map shows where Protoceratops fossils have been found.

Key to map

Protoceratops fossils

NORTH

NORTH AMERICA

SOUTH AMERICA

In 1922, photographer J. B. Shackelford found the first Protoceratops fossil. He found a skull in the Gobi Desert, in Mongolia. Many bones and eggs have been found since then.

Where Did Protoceratops Live?

Protoceratops lived in sandy deserts. These deserts had large hills of sand formed by the wind, called dunes. They also had some streams and lakes.

Protoceratops had to find water to drink so it could survive in its desert home.

dunes

The deserts where Protoceratops lived had a hot and dry **climate**, just like most deserts today. Only tough plants, such as cycads and palms, could grow.

What Did Protoceratops Eat?

Protoceratops was a herbivore, or plant-eater. It cut pieces off tough plants with its beak. It then chewed them up using its strong jaws and sharp teeth.

Foods Eaten by Protoceratops	
Cycads	
Palms	

Protoceratops may have found food near streams or rivers because more plants grow near water. It may also have fed on plants as it walked to new places.

Protoceratops probably found enough plants to eat by staying near water.

Predator or Prey?

Protoceratops was **prey** for a meat-eating dinosaur called Velociraptor (*ve-loss-uh-rap-tor*). Protoceratops would have had trouble defending itself against this small, fierce **predator**.

Protoceratops was too heavy to run quickly and was probably easy prey for Velociraptor.

Protoceratops protected itself from predators by living in a herd, or group. When a predator attacked, there was less chance that each Protoceratops would be caught.

In a herd, there was a good chance that at least one Protoceratops would have seen an approaching predator and could warn the others.

How Did Protoceratops Live?

Paleontologists think Protoceratops lived in a herd. This is because they have found many skeletons and nests close together.

Protoceratops may have displayed its neck frill to others in the herd to show how important it was.

Protoceratops probably spent its time eating plants. It moved somewhere new when it had eaten all of the plants in an area.

Protoceratops may have had to walk long distances to find fresh plants to eat.

Life Cycle of Protoceratops

Paleontologists study fossils and living animals to learn about the life cycle of Protoceratops.

1. An adult male Protoceratops displayed his neck frill to attract a female. The male and female **mated**.

4. Baby Protoceratops left the nest soon after hatching. They grew into adults.

They believe there were four main stages in the life cycle of Protoceratops. This is what it may have been like.

2. The female laid long, thin eggs in a shallow nest in soft, dry sand. Several females built nests near each other.

3. Baby Protoceratops hatched from the eggs. Their mothers brought them plants to eat for a few days.

What Happened to Protoceratops?

Protoceratops became **extinct** about 80 million years ago. Some paleontologists believe that herds died out during heat waves or because they were buried under sand.

buried nests

Baby Protoceratops would not have survived if their nests were buried under sand.

The last dinosaurs became extinct about 65 million years ago. Many paleontologists think dinosaurs died out when a large **meteorite** hit Earth. Others think **climate change** or volcanoes caused their extinction.

Protoceratops could not survive changing conditions on Earth, leaving us with only fossils.

Names and Their Meanings

Dinosaurs are named by people who discover them or paleontologists who study them. A dinosaur may be named for its appearance or behavior. Its name may also honor a person or place.

Name	Meaning
Dinosaur	Terrible lizard—because people thought dinosaurs were powerful lizards
Ankylosaurus	Fused lizard—because many of its bones were joined together
Diplodocus	Double beam—because it had special bones in its tail
Muttaburrasaurus	Muttaburra lizard—because it was discovered near the town of Muttaburra, in Australia
Protoceratops	First horned face—because it was one of the early horned dinosaurs
Tyrannosaurus	Tyrant lizard—because it was a fearsome ruler of the land
Velociraptor	Speedy thief—because it ran quickly and ate meat

Glossary

climate — The usual weather in a place.

climate change — Changes in the usual weather in a place

extinct — No longer existing.

mated — Created offspring.

meteorite — A rock from space that has landed on Earth.

predator — An animal that hunts and kills other animals for food.

prey — An animal that is hunted and killed by other animals for food.

reptiles — Creeping or crawling animals that are covered with scales.

sense — A special ability that people and animals use to experience the world around them. Typically, those senses are sight, hearing, smell, taste, and touch.

skeletons — The bones inside the body of a person or an animal.

Index

B
beak, 13, 14, 20
bird-hipped dinosaurs, 6, 7, 10
brain, 14

C
Cretaceous period, 5, 11

D
deserts, 17, 18, 19

E
eggs, 8, 17, 27
extinction, 28, 29

F
food, 7, 15, 20, 21
fossils, 8, 9, 16–17, 26, 29

H
herbivores, 20

J
Jurassic period, 5, 11

L
life cycle, 26–27
lizard-hipped dinosaurs, 6, 7

M
meat-eating dinosaurs, 7, 22, 30
Mesozoic Era, 5, 11

N
neck frill, 10, 13, 14, 24, 26

P
paleontologists, 9, 24, 26, 28, 29, 30
plant-eating dinosaurs, 7, 10, 20, 21, 25, 27
predators, 22, 23
prey, 22

R
reptiles, 4

S
senses, 15
skeletons, 9, 24
skin, 13
skulls, 7, 14, 17

T
tail, 13, 30
teeth, 8, 14, 20
Triassic period, 5, 11